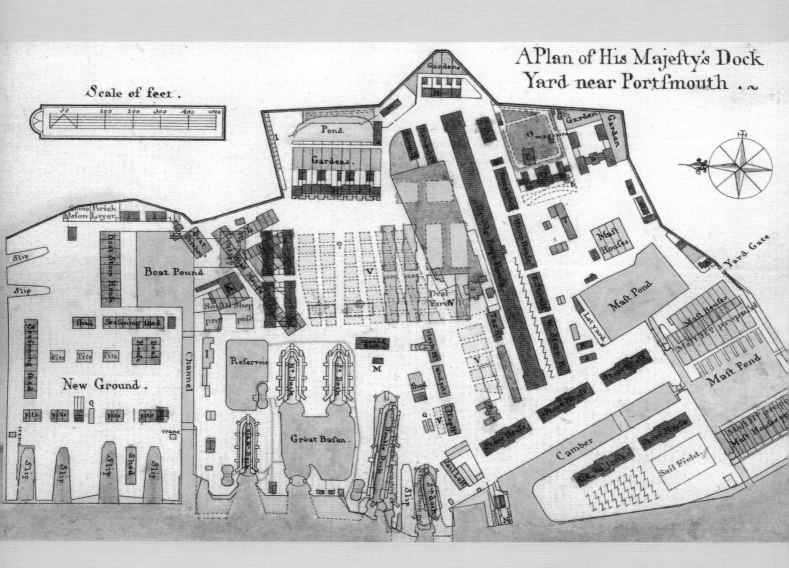

A Plan of His Majesty's Dock Yard near Portsmouth.

Scale of feet.

Many of the features marked on this plan of 1786 still survive today, including the impressive 1,095-foot-long rope house.

Going home through Victory Gate around 1900.

HISTORY OF PORTSMOUTH ROYAL DOCKYARD

Portsmouth Dockyard has a long and distinguished history. Home to the world's first dry dock, built in 1495, the dockyard rose to national prominence. In 1510 the keel of the *Mary Rose* was laid there and two years later Portsmouth was officially appointed a building centre for the King's ships. No visible traces of the medieval dockyard remain, but the original dry dock lies under the Great Ship Basin, near HMS *Victory*.

During a period of almost continuous naval warfare in the 18th and early 19th centuries, the dockyard developed into the largest industrial complex in the world, reaching a peak with the opening of the Blockmills in 1803. The world's first steam-powered factory produced pulley blocks that were essential for the rigging and gun carriages on ships like HMS *Victory*. Interspersed between the industrial and office buildings, the dockyard was a town within a town, with houses, churches, schools, a mortuary, shops, surgeries and a fire station.

↑ At their peak the Blockmills turned out 130,000 pulley blocks annually.

↓ The first of three Georgian storehouses built between 1764 and 1784.

Construction of the Victorian dockyard extension saw builders remove three times more spoil than for the Channel Tunnel.

Innovation in ship design from sail to steam in the 19th century necessitated dramatic changes to the dockyard, leading to the construction of a huge steam basin together with three dry docks, and engine and boiler factories on land to the north of the existing dockyard. A crowd of 15,000 watched as Queen Victoria opened the new complex in 1848. At the time one of the biggest and most modern naval facilities in the world, within 15 years it had become outdated as warships grew rapidly in size prompting a further massive expansion programme.

The early 20th century saw the construction of the great battleship HMS *Dreadnought*, which was completed in the astonishing time of 366 days. This ship generated huge worldwide interest and sparked a shipbuilding race as tensions rose prior to the First World War and Britain sought to maintain her naval supremacy.

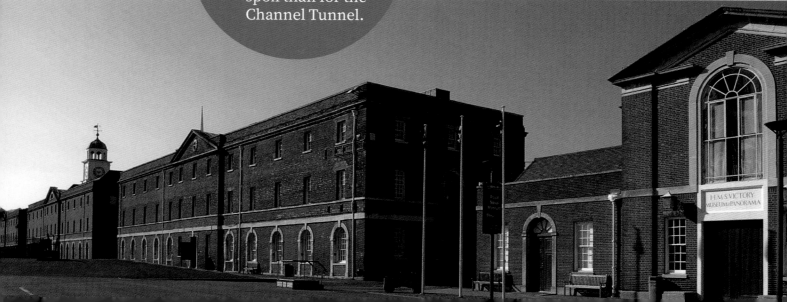

←← Dockyard fire and policemen pose outside the fire station built in 1843.

← The crew of HMS *Wasp* in the 1860s.

↓ Another Portsmouth-built ship slides down the slip.

H.M.S "NEPTUNE" TAKING HER BAPTISM SILK, 2

The Porter's Garden, in the grounds of the oldest building in the dockyard (built 1708).

HMS *Queen Elizabeth*, built at Portsmouth in 1913.

The dockyard's strategic importance throughout the Second World War meant it was a prime target for German bombers and it suffered severe damage. The post-war years brought a reduction in the Navy, but its role was slowly changing and the dockyard was kept busy modernising the fleet to meet the new nuclear and missile age. Following the outbreak of the Falklands War in 1982, the dockyard worked round the clock to refit the task force and load stores, ammunition and fuel.

Today, Portsmouth Dockyard continues to be of prime importance to the Royal Navy. The home port for 60 per cent of the fleet, the dockyard has also contributed to the construction of the massive new Queen Elizabeth-class carriers, which will be based here from 2017.

→ The crew of HMS *Zanzibar* in the 1940s.

↘ HMS *Daring* berthed close to HMS *Victory*.

There were over 23 miles of railway track running through the dockyard. Some of the old track is visible in places.

THE MARY ROSE

The *Mary Rose*'s long and remarkable history enters an exciting new phase in 2016 as The Mary Rose Museum, in which the Tudor ship is housed, enhances its visitor experience. The wall that previously separated visitors from the ship has been replaced with glazing, offering spectacular unrestricted views. You can now appreciate the full magnitude of the ship for the first time since she was raised from the Solent in 1982.

Painstakingly preserved over 34 years, the *Mary Rose* is the only 16th-century warship on display in the world. Set within a museum that reunites the ship with many of her artefacts and crew, it is a unique time capsule giving an insight into life on board a Tudor warship.

Built for Henry VIII in 1510, the *Mary Rose* fought battles against the French for over 30 years. When she capsized off the coast of Portsmouth on 19 July 1545, during the Battle of the Solent, it looked like she was lost forever, along with most of the 500 men on board. Despite strenuous attempts to salvage the ship, she remained on the seabed.

← Raising the hull of the *Mary Rose* from the Solent on 10 October 1982.

↓ Until 2016, large air ducts helped dry the timbers of the ship.

Mary Rose served Henry VIII for 34 years and it has taken 34 years to conserve her.

The ship's bell that rings every half an hour in the museum is actually a recording of the real Mary Rose bell.

A bronze gun in the Main Deck Context gallery.

For centuries the *Mary Rose* lay on her starboard side, leaving the port side exposed to the Solent currents and marine organisms. However, over time, the ship was covered with a layer of silt, which fortunately protected her from further erosion.

Rediscovered more than 400 years later, the complicated and delicate task of salvage commenced. Archaeologists and volunteer divers spent years excavating every centimetre of the ship, using their hands and small trowels to uncover precious artefacts.

An impressive collection of nearly 19,000 items were recovered, most of which are now on display in the museum. These include personal belongings such as wooden bowls, leather shoes, musical instruments and nit combs, together with many of the ship's weapons, from longbows to two-ton guns. The museum also offers a unique insight into the life of crew members, with forensic science used to reveal their stories.

↖ Nit combs to bowls: some of the many artefacts removed from the ship.

↑ Hatch, the ship's dog.

← The *Mary Rose* under sail, painted by Geoff Hunt.

Based on evidence from paint samples the hull has now been painted a paler colour.

HMS VICTORY

There have been many celebrated warships in Britain's naval history but HMS *Victory* can justifiably claim to be the most famous of them all. Having served as Vice Admiral Lord Nelson's flagship at the Battle of Trafalgar, she has become one of the UK's most cherished visitor attractions.

The death of Nelson on board *Victory* during the Battle of Trafalgar is an iconic moment in history. The Vice Admiral was fatally shot on 21 October 1805 by a French sailor in the mizzen mast of *La Redoubtable*. After being shot, Nelson was carried to the Orlop Deck, where many other injured seamen and officers were awaiting medical attention. Three hours later he was dead but a British victory was assured.

Less well known is *Victory*'s earlier history. First floated out in 1765, *Victory* spent 13 years in reserve at Chatham before going on to become one of the most successful naval ships of all time, leading fleets in a series of history-changing wars, including the American War of Independence and the Napoleonic War.

Around 6,000 trees were cut down to build HMS *Victory*.

Victory's guns had gunlocks, which gave a faster and more accurate aim than those of her opponents at the Battle of Trafalgar.

The Main Gun Deck.

At the age of 40, *Victory* achieved lasting fame at the Battle of Trafalgar. Yet, even after her finest hour, she went on to further service in the Baltic and other seas before her career as a fighting ship ended in 1812. Coincidentally, she was 47 years old, the same age Nelson had been when he died.

After years moored in Portsmouth Harbour, *Victory* was saved for posterity in 1922 following a national appeal and placed into dry dock at Portsmouth Historic Dockyard.

In 2016 *Victory* saw the biggest change to the way she is presented to the public since 1928, with a major reinterpretation of the visitor route through the ship. Visitors can now follow in the footsteps of Nelson, her most famous Admiral, from the time the ship embarks on her defining voyage to Cape Trafalgar, to the aftermath of the fearsome battle with the French.

HMS WARRIOR 1860

HMS *Warrior* was launched on 29 December 1860 and was, at that time, the fastest, largest and most powerful warship in the world. Such was the technical and warfighting innovation invested in her that potential enemies were intimidated by her obvious supremacy – but she never fired a shot in anger.

HMS *Warrior* was Great Britain's response to France's launch of *La Gloire* in 1859, the world's first ocean-going, iron-clad warship. At a time of rumours of French invasion, she and her sister ship, HMS *Black Prince*, were built as deterrents. Their thick, armour-plated sides offered defence against the new exploding shells; their high speed under both sail and steam, and large guns protected within a citadel, gave them evident battle supremacy over any other warship in the world. HMS *Warrior* entered active service in 1862 amidst great public fanfare, and her reputation spread quickly at home and overseas.

↑ Laid ready for dinner: sailors ate at the mess tables between the guns.

↓ *Warrior*'s boiler room.

HMS Warrior was the first warship to have top-loading washing machines.

→ The nominated cook of each mess prepared the main midday meal in the galley.

Rapid advances in naval technologies post-1860 included the introduction of armoured gun turrets, improvements in steam machinery and industrial metal production. Ironically, many of these developments were inspired by *Warrior*'s creation, but they meant the ship herself became obsolete quite quickly. By 1871 she was transferred to coastguard and reserve services, and in 1904 was converted to a floating school and renamed *Vernon III*.

In 1924 she was put up for sale as scrap but no buyer could be found. Five years later she was converted into a floating refuelling pontoon at Pembroke Dock and renamed *Oil Fuel Hulk C77*.

Following the closure of the oil depot in 1978, she was acquired by the Manifold Trust for saving as the last surviving member of Queen Victoria's renowned Black Battle Fleet. *Warrior* was restored in Hartlepool to her original presentation on launch. She returned triumphantly to Portsmouth on 16 June 1987 and has since remained on public display as a living ship, providing visitors with an insight into life on board an elite warship from the Victorian era.

HMS M.33

HMS *M.33* is one of only two Royal Navy warships to survive from the First World War and the only one from the Gallipoli Campaign.

Built on the orders of First Lord of the Admiralty Winston Churchill, she was part of a new fleet of small 'monitor' gunships designed to operate in shallow coastal waters.

Constructed in just seven weeks, the ship was soon heading into action. Arriving at Turkey's Gallipoli Peninsula in July 1915, *M.33* was just in time to support a major Allied offensive designed to break the deadlock of the land campaign. During an intense eight-day period the crew fired 316 shells on the Turkish gun batteries which were bombarding the right flank of the Australian and New Zealand Army Corps (ANZAC). Thereafter, the ship conducted regular patrols until the Allied evacuation in January 1916.

HMS *M.33* remained in the Aegean Sea for the rest of the war, supporting Allied forces against the Bulgarians at Salonika in 1916 and undertaking various bombardment, blockade and patrol duties. As she lost no crew to enemy action she gained a reputation as a 'lucky' ship.

↑ The aft gun was replaced during the restoration programme. Originally from HMS *Canada*, it saw action at the Battle of Jutland in 1916.

↓ *M.33*'s crew in 1915.

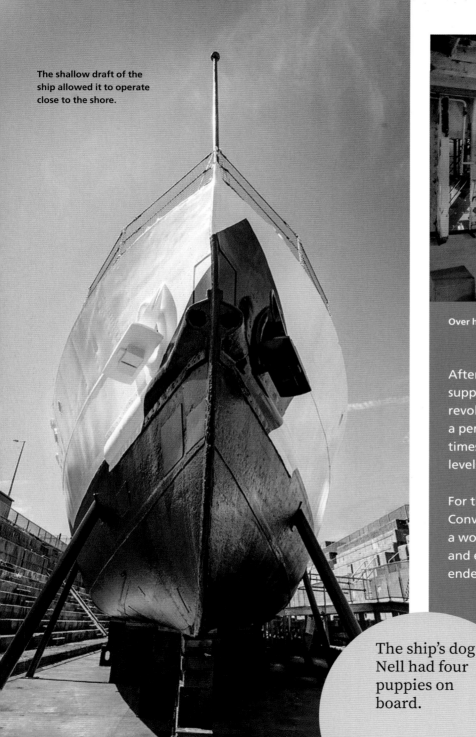

The shallow draft of the ship allowed it to operate close to the shore.

The ship's dog Nell had four puppies on board.

Over half the crew lived in the For'ard Mess Deck.

After a brief return to England in 1919, *M.33* supported forces opposing Lenin's Bolshevik revolutionaries on the River Dvina in Russia. During a perilous three-month period the ship was hit five times and became grounded when the river's water levels fell – but she survived.

For the next 65 years *M.33* carried out various roles. Converted into a minelayer, a tender (transfer ship), a workshop for boom defences (anti-submarine nets) and eventually a floating office, her naval life finally ended in 1984.

In 2015 a major programme of conservation of the ship was completed. Much of the original fabric of the vessel has been preserved and, in places, restored to reflect her original purpose.

The Grand Fleet at sea.

The Morning News
Saturday June 3rd

GREAT
NAVAL
BATTLE
HUGE BRITISH AND
GERMAN LOSSES

Survivors on the hospital ship *Plassy*.

36 HOURS: JUTLAND 1916
THE BATTLE THAT WON THE WAR

In May 1916 the fleets of the Imperial German and Royal Navies fought the defining naval battle of the First World War – the Battle of Jutland.

To mark the centenary, the National Museum of the Royal Navy is hosting a special exhibition in Boathouse 5. It puts visitors at the heart of the action and combines dramatic audio visual experiences with many unique historical artefacts associated with the battle. The exhibition includes items from public and private collections across the UK and is a unique opportunity to view artefacts never before seen together. Many are on display to the public for the first time.

Integral to the exhibition are the stories of individuals, both British and German, who witnessed the events unfold. Their accounts reveal the drama and confusion of warfare at sea and encourage reflection on the impact of the battle in the immediate aftermath and its long-term legacy.

HMS *Centurion* flies her ensigns on the way to the battle.

Medals awarded to Lt Col Jones, HMS *Lion*.

NATIONAL MUSEUM OF THE ROYAL NAVY PORTSMOUTH

The Royal Navy has helped to shape the world. It made Britain a dominant sea-power, protected its trade in troubled times, defended it from invasion or carried the attack overseas. The Royal Navy has touched the lives of millions of people worldwide, from service personnel and their families to those who built, serviced and supplied its ships and influenced the lives of communities overseas.

The National Museum of the Royal Navy, Portsmouth brings this history to life, showcasing treasures from the past 350 years. Personal stories are used to explore the key events and examine the changes, as well as common threads, which link the sailor of the sailing-era Navy to the professional modern crews of today.

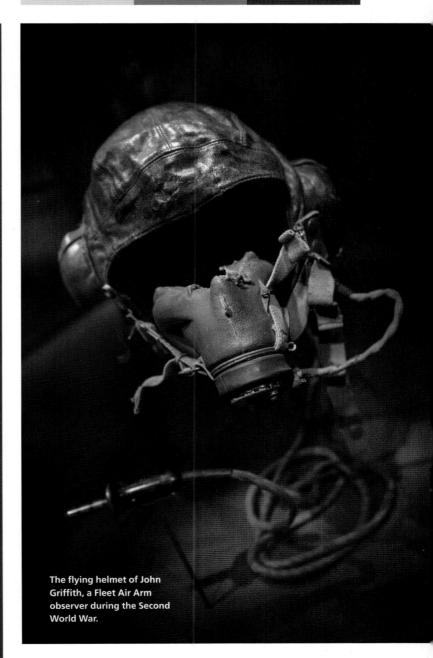

The flying helmet of John Griffith, a Fleet Air Arm observer during the Second World War.

The SAILING NAVY

The museum contains the world's oldest Christmas pudding. Given to sailors fighting in the Boer War in 1900, it has remained uneaten.

A model of HMS *Eagle*.

A gun from HMS *Lance*.

Families' day on HMS *Queen Elizabeth* in 1919.

The museum's major gallery, HMS *Hear My Story*, features the stories of men and women who have shaped the Navy's amazing history over the last 100 years – the century of greatest change. Cutting-edge interpretation allows the visitor to see and hear accounts of the Navy in war and peacetime, from the storms of the Arctic to the heat of Afghanistan. Visitors can hunt a submarine, send a message in code or meet veterans who will share their stories of living and fighting at sea.

Next door, the museum's exhibitions focus on the 18th and 19th centuries. The Sailing Navy exhibition conveys the realities of fighting at sea in the age of sail, while Nelson: The Hero and the Man examines Nelson's colourful but short life.

The Sir Donald Gosling Victory Gallery explores the history of Britain's most famous warship from the laying of her keel to her significant battles. Here, visitors can walk through the multimedia Trafalgar Experience, meeting Nelson and his great foe Napoleon and feel the blast of the Main Gun Deck during the battle. As HMS *Victory* undergoes her most extensive refit since Trafalgar, the exhibitions will reveal the forensic analysis changing our understanding of *Victory*'s past and the scientific investigations showing new ways of securing her future.

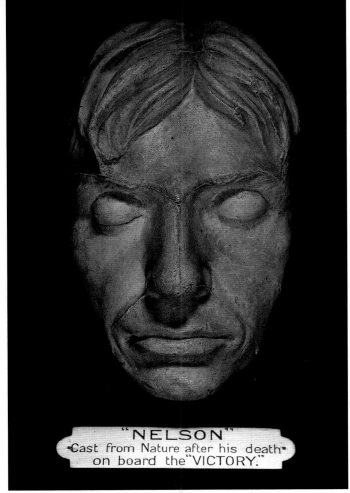

"NELSON"
Cast from Nature after his death
on board the "VICTORY."

The multimedia Trafalgar Experience.

WORKMEN LEAVING MUSTER STATION.
PORTSMOUTH DOCKYARD. 4.

TOPIC

Mary Lacy disguised herself as a man in order to get her shipwright's certificate, which she achieved in 1770.

James Nasmyth's huge steam hammer, installed in 1845.

DOCKYARD APPRENTICE EXHIBITION

Following in the footsteps of generations of dockyard apprentices, visitors clock in after passing through the dockyard wall and, with the help of many interactive exhibits, learn about the wide variety of skills and crafts essential for building and maintaining the British fleet.

Competition for apprenticeships was fierce. Those boys, and from 1969 girls, who passed the entrance exam undertook classroom study and practical work in their chosen trade. At the end of their apprenticeship – as long as seven years at the start of the 20th century, but eventually reduced to four years – they would submit a test piece showcasing their skills in order to qualify as a skilled craftsperson.

The Admiralty Apprenticeship Scheme ensured there was a steady replenishment of skilled people into the workforce. At its peak during the Second World War, the dockyard employed around 45,000 men and women.

The exhibition is located within Boathouse 7. Situated above the mast pond this building originally housed a specialist mast-making facility.

A recreation of workers repairing a boat.

BOATHOUSE 4

Restored in 2015, Boathouse 4 is a cathedral-sized family attraction within the Historic Dockyard, with exhibitions, hands-on activities and a brand-new indoor mast-climbing experience.

At its heart is the Boatbuilding and Heritage Skills Centre, which reflects the building's original use as a small boatbuilding and repair facility. Today, it is home to both the International Boatbuilding College Portsmouth and Highbury College, each of which offers a range of practical courses in traditional boatbuilding techniques ensuring that these time-honoured skills are kept alive for future generations. Visitors can watch students in action and are actively encouraged to have a go themselves.

Dramatically suspended from the ceiling, and displayed on the mezzanine above, is a collection of small historic boats in the Forgotten Craft exhibition. This display tells the stories of the small vessels that were the backbone of the Royal Navy, from the wooden cutters that ferried Lord Nelson to and from his flagship, to the Cockleshell Heroes in their canoes and the powerful motor boats that helped to win the Second World War. One of the most impressive is the landing craft from HMS *Fearless* used during the Falklands War.

↑ A display of ships' badges in the Midships Cookhouse.
↓ A stack of portholes await refitting.

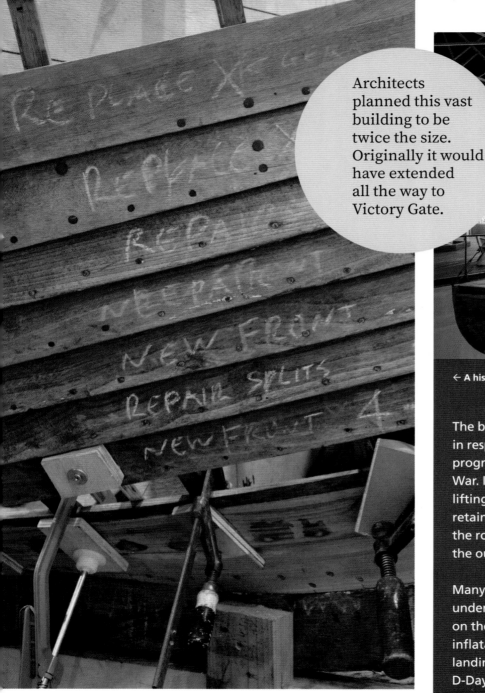

Architects planned this vast building to be twice the size. Originally it would have extended all the way to Victory Gate.

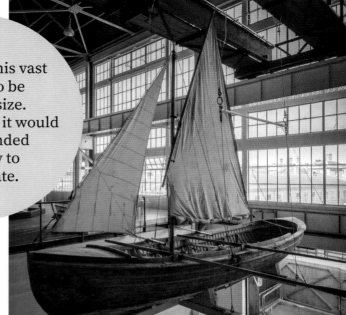

← A historic boat undergoes repair.

The building itself was hastily constructed in 1939 in response to the need for a rapid rearmament programme prior to the start of the Second World War. Indeed, the massive overhead cranes used for lifting boats in and out of the dock and locks still retain a camouflage paint scheme, necessary because the roof of the building had not been completed at the outbreak of war.

Many experimental and top-secret projects were undertaken here during the war. These included work on the first prototype midget submarines and trials for inflatable lifting bags, which could be used to repair landing craft on the Normandy beaches following the D-Day landings.

↓ Looking down on activity in the main boat repair area.

↓ The Forgotten Craft exhibition.

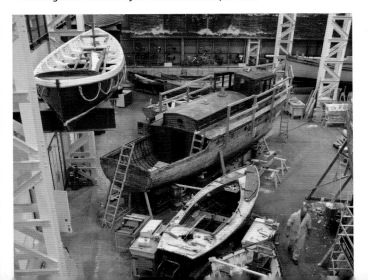

ACTION STATIONS

Built between 1845 and 1848, Boathouse 6 was once at the forefront of design and innovation in the Victorian era. It now houses Action Stations, a high-tech, interactive indoor attraction, which features a unique series of physical challenges, simulators and technological experiments, putting visitors at the heart of the modern naval experience.

Originally, the building's primary purpose was to repair and maintain small craft known as 'ship's boats'. These small vessels served the larger ships in the fleet, such as HMS *Victory*, which at the time were too large to enter the dockyard and had to anchor in the Solent, at Spithead. Hundreds of ship's boats were needed to ferry sailors to and from the dockyard, and to load and unload supplies and cargo.

Have you got what it takes to face the Ninja Force? Action Stations' new assault course opens in 2016.

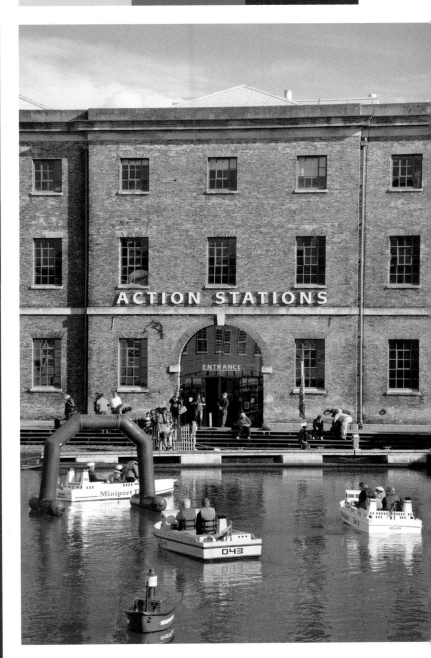

Boathouse 6 was the largest maintenance building of its kind. Boats were hauled up the slipway from the mast pond through the three huge doors at the front, before being hoisted to the first floor for repairs.

During the Second World War, the building took direct hits to the first and second floors and was roughly patched up by the Royal Navy. Following the war its usefulness diminished and it gradually fell into disrepair until work began in 1998 to turn Boathouse 6 into the state-of-the-art attraction we see today.

**HMS *Dragon* and HMS *Illustrious*
in Portsmouth Harbour.**

HARBOUR TOUR AND WATERBUS

Portsmouth Harbour has been of key importance to naval forces for over 1,200 years, but it was in 1194 that King Richard I granted Portsmouth a Royal Charter to construct a dockyard.

Portsmouth is still home to the Royal Navy and taking the Harbour Tour is the best way to appreciate the size and scale of its impressive fleet of ships. The tour offers unrivalled views of Britain's modern frigates, destroyers and other vessels, as well as historic buildings and the dramatic skyline of the harbour.

During the Harbour Tour visitors can see many of the fortifications that were built to protect Portsmouth Dockyard over the centuries. The Round Tower at the harbour entrance and the Solent forts that formed the centre of a string of defences along the coast during the Napoleonic Wars, are of particular interest.

The Waterbus allows visitors to hop across the water from the Historic Dockyard to visit both the Royal Navy Submarine Museum and Explosion Museum of Naval Firepower in Gosport.

↓ HMS *Dauntless*.

The densely packed control room of HMS *Alliance*, with the periscope in the foreground and the chart table behind.

ROYAL NAVY SUBMARINE MUSEUM

A striking symbol of submarine history, HMS *Alliance* served the Royal Navy for over 28 years and stands as a memorial to the 5,300 British submariners who have lost their lives in service.

Launched in 1945, *Alliance* was one of 14 A-class long-range submarines built for service in the Far East. In 1958 she was modified for Cold War duties. Her low conning tower and anti-aircraft guns were replaced with a fin that completely covered her periscopes making her faster and quieter.

Home to 65 officers and men, the guided tour offers a taste of their lives at sea. Visitors see their cramped accommodation and control room spaces, before squeezing past the galley to the aft torpedo compartment. Portsmouth Harbour can even be viewed through working periscopes.

HMS *Alliance* forms the centrepiece of the Royal Navy Submarine Museum, along with *Holland I* (Britain's first submarine) and *X24* (the only surviving British midget submarine from the Second World War). The museum's unique collection also contains thousands of photographs, ship plans and artefacts telling the story of the submarine service.

↑ The crew of HMS *Alliance*.

The torpedo tubes were sometimes used for keeping the crew's beer cold!

Workers at Priddy's Hard wore special clothing and shoes to prevent sparks igniting the explosives they handled.

A display of shells in the Big Guns Gallery.

EXPLOSION MUSEUM OF NAVAL FIREPOWER

Housed in a former Royal Naval Ordnance Depot, Explosion is an interactive museum telling the story of naval warfare together with the stories of the thousands of men and women who worked at Priddy's Hard.

During the Napoleonic Wars all Royal Navy warships, including HMS *Victory*, came to load up ammunition from here. Barrels of gunpowder were rolled to the harbour edge, loaded onto small boats called 'powder hoys' and transferred to the ships. Located a safe distance from the main dockyard, the site could store up to 6,500 barrels.

In the 1850s, a series of large magazines was built to fill and store shells for the new breech-loading guns. By the 1880s, the replacement of gunpowder with highly explosive cordite as a propellant in shells prompted the building of a narrow gauge railway to transport ordnance between the filling and storage buildings.

The site continued to evolve with the introduction of new explosives and technologies up to the arrival of guided missiles in the 1960s, when it went into decline. The last time the site supplied weapons to the Navy was in 1982 for the Falklands War.

↑ **Weighing the explosives charges.**

Traditionally, Marines used the left-hand stair in the mess to avoid looking at Charity, who featured above the other stair.

ROYAL MARINES MUSEUM

The Royal Marines Museum is housed in the historic Victorian barracks at Eastney. Here, visitors can journey through 350 years of naval history, tracing the story of the Royal Navy's elite fighting force from their inception in 1664 during the reign of Charles II to the formation of the Royal Marine Commandos in 1942 and up to the present day.

Throughout their history the Royal Marines have proudly served at the forefront of numerous conflicts, including the Battle of Trafalgar, both World Wars, the Falklands War, and the 21st-century conflicts in Iraq and Afghanistan. Featured throughout the museum are the personal stories of the personnel involved, such as that of Hannah Snell, who ran away to sea in 1745 and joined the Royal Marines as a man.

The family-friendly museum also offers hands-on interactive games, simulators, and sight, sound and touch experiences. The Making of a Royal Marine Commando exhibition invites visitors to follow in the footsteps of a recruit during training. Other galleries allow them to creep through the jungle or experience First World War trench warfare on the Western Front. They can then end their visit by tackling the assault course outside or climbing on board the rigid raider.

← 'The Yomper' by Philip Jackson at the museum entrance.

↓ Memorial trumpets and drums commemorating losses in the First World War.